MW00490813

I'M ADDICTED

Jim Berg

Consulting Editor: Dr. Paul Tautges

Help! I'm Addicted

© 2020 Palmetto Services Upstate, LLC

ISBN
Paper: 978-1-63342-210-0
epub: 978-1-63342-211-7
Kindle: 978-1-63342-212-4

Published by **Shepherd Press**
P.O. Box 24
Wapwallopen, PA 18660

www.shepherdpress.com

All Scripture quotations, unless stated otherwise, are from the ESV 2016.

Designed by **documen**

CONTENTS

INTRODUCTION

You've heard the stories and read the stats. Marijuana use and vaping are taking the teen population by storm. Almost one-third of all auto fatalities are alcohol related. Opioid abuse has reached crisis proportions, and daily fentanyl overdoses continue to skyrocket. Eating disorders, self-injury, and other self-destructive behaviors are on the rise. Every family is touched by addiction in some way. Everybody knows somebody who is addicted to something.

But addiction is more personal for you, isn't it? You have your own story. You aren't a statistic. You are not a number. You are a person who once had real hopes and dreams, real desires and wishes, and real possibilities.

But then you became addicted.

Maybe it started when you tried to numb the pain of traumatic events or of a dysfunctional upbringing by self-medicating with alcohol or painkillers or cutting. Maybe it started because you wanted to impress your friends by joining their party scene, or maybe it started because you wanted to experience a drug-induced high *just once* to see what it was like.

But no matter how it started, once wasn't enough, was it? There always seemed to be good reasons to smoke another joint, snort another hit, visit another casino, meet another coworker for after-work drinks and sex, restrict yourself in order to lose one more pound, start another food binge-and-purge episode, or explore another porn site on the Internet. What started out as a fun-filled fling or an attempt at some momentary relief from pain and shame grew into something bigger. You started hiding, lying, isolating, or becoming bolder and more daring—and more dangerous. You may have burned your relational bridges, begun destroying your health, and hurt the people who love you the most.

Maybe you were arrested, or lost your job, your driver's license, your savings, or even your family. Maybe it was then, at that moment, that you realized you were *hooked*. That's a descriptive word, isn't it? You feel like a fish that can't get loose from the angler's line because you are caught and, struggle as you will, you feel as if you are being *reeled in*. You fear that the end will be your destruction.

Let me assure you right from the start that no matter how tangled your life has become, *God offers hope and help through his Word and his people.*

1

What Is Addiction?

Before we look at some definitions of addiction, let me introduce you to Sam,[1] a dear friend of mine. Sam was twenty-two years old when he was arrested again for driving under the influence and for possessing narcotics. He had used many different street drugs and had been on something most of the time for several years. But having a cell door slam shut in his face that night had not been on his bucket list.

Sam's Turbulent Journey

As a young boy, Sam occasionally attended a small brick church in his neighborhood. He had heard the gospel message about how Christ came to save sinners—and he now had no doubt that he was one (Romans 3:23). That night in his cell, he remembered the pastor's words that Christ died to pay the penalty for sin and rose from the dead (Romans 4:25; 5:8), and that God would accept sinners who repented of their sin and placed their faith in Jesus Christ as their only Savior (Romans 6:23). Sin had carried him farther than he had ever expected. He fell on his face on the cold concrete floor of his cell and cried out to God for mercy and forgiveness (Romans 10:9).

That's when Sam's new life began. Before long he was spending hours a day in his cell reading the Bible he found on a bookshelf in the study room next to the canteen. He detoxed in jail, completed his ninety-day sentence, was released on probation, and awaited another trial for previous offenses. He knew that he really needed to be on a faith-based resident program so that he could learn more about his new Savior, Jesus Christ, who could rescue him from the destructive ways of his past.

Six months later Sam graduated from a resident addiction-recovery discipleship program, where the Bible-saturated schedule, one-on-one discipleship, Christian community, and strict accountability gave him the head start he needed on the path to victory over his stubborn, sinful habits.

He joined a Bible-believing church and began attending their Friday night addiction-recovery discipleship program, Freedom That Lasts.[2] There he gained a whole new "family" of fellow believers who accepted him, loved him, helped him find a job, discipled him, and prayed for him—all within the context of God's "support group," the brothers and sisters of a local church.

Then one day Sam learned that someone he dearly loved had died. Sam relapsed into his old ways of handling pain—he did drugs. Under the influence of heroin that night he wrecked his car and was arrested for DUI. He was released on bail and within a few weeks was again standing before a judge who placed him under house arrest until his other cases could come before the court. This time he knew he had to learn to handle pain God's way.

Though Sam is now walking in joy and victory, he still faces an uncertain future legally and has incurred some very difficult relational and financial responsibilities due to his previous choices. Yet, by placing himself back under the instruction, accountability, and community of his church, he is developing a consistent walk with God, sharing his testimony with others, and becoming a responsible employee.

His house-arrest restrictions allow him to go only to work, church, and home again to the transition house he shares with several other men. The GPS in his ankle bracelet would betray him to the monitoring agency if he were to veer off course. Since he can't run around like he did before, he has plenty of time to devote to reading and studying his Bible, listening to sermon podcasts, and reading books on Christian growth. Every day his ankle bracelet reminds him that he must deny himself and remain under the limitations that God (through the penal system, Romans 13:1–7) has placed upon him in order to develop the character of Christ. He still has setbacks, but he is learning to handle hurts and hardships in a far different manner than he did before. He's developing biblical wisdom.

What did Sam have to learn in order to become a different kind of person? We will look at the answer to that question in chapter 2, but first we need to clarify what addiction really is.

Definitions of Addiction

The American Society of Addictive Medicine defines addiction as

> *a treatable, chronic medical disease involving complex interactions among brain circuits, genetics, the environment, and an individual's life experiences* [emphasis mine].[3]

Addiction certainly *feels* like a disease because sometimes it seems as if you *can't help* doing it again, just as you can't help vomiting if you have a stomach virus. However, while the concept of disease may help illustrate how addiction *feels*, it doesn't accurately explain how addiction *starts*. You can't get an addiction from bacteria, a virus, or a parasite you picked up somewhere.

Many secular addiction specialists also disagree with the disease model. For example, neuroscientist and developmental psychologist Marc Lewis in his book *The Biology of Desire: Why Addiction Is Not a Disease* states that

> *medical researchers are correct that the brain changes with addiction. But the way it changes has to do with learning and development—not disease.*[4]

Lewis asserts that

> *addiction results . . . from the motivated repetition of the same thoughts and behaviors until they become habitual.*[5]

When you choose to repeat a pleasurable experience, your body (and your brain, which is part of your body) adjusts to desire it more. Your brain begins to shut out other thoughts and goals so that you can focus more intently on getting the "high" you chose initially and then kept choosing. The greater the emotional pleasure from your choices and the more you repeat those choices, the more quickly your body begins to crave them again. *These bodily changes take place because God made your body to be the servant of your heart.* Once wrongly "trained" by a misguided heart, your body has to be "retrained" as your heart thinks new thoughts, develops new desires, and learns new strategies for handling life.

Interestingly, brain scans of heroin addicts are identical to the brain scans of newly married people. Both experience repeated behaviors which produce a high level of pleasure or euphoria. This is good news for the newly married couple because their brains and body chemistry begin reinforcing their commitment to each other. It is bad news, however, when the repeated behavior is sinful. It leads to slavery, and because you personally chose to begin and continue the behavior, you must consider your addictions as *"voluntary* slavery."[6] We can call them *life-dominating sins* or *stubborn sinful habits*.

Most treatments today focus largely upon the physical components of addiction—detox or replacement drug therapy (like methadone). Some treatment programs add behavioral modification through stress- and anger-management programs and classes on coping skills. While these can bring some relief (even sobriety) and are welcome changes for the addict's family and friends, they can never help you become everything God created you to be because they ignore the most important component of a fulfilling life—God!

We All Have a Dependency "Disorder"[7]

You might wonder why you need God in your life. Let me explain. Your battle with addiction is not merely a *physical* dependency upon substances and behaviors. There is something bigger going on here. Living in a fallen, broken world introduces all kinds of hurts and disappointments into your life, and you have chosen to handle them your own way.

The biggest choice you have in life is this: *On whom will you depend to enable you to handle the setbacks of life—God or yourself?* Will you choose to put your trust in your own ideas and strategies for getting relief from the pain, or will you acknowledge your need for relationship with God and for wisdom from him? Because you choose to depend on yourself instead of God to solve life's hurts and hardships, we could say that you have a *dependency disorder*. You have replaced God and his ways with your own ways. Think carefully about this passage of Scripture:

> Trust in the LORD with all your heart,
>   and do not lean on your own understanding.
> In all your ways acknowledge him,
>   and he will make straight your paths.
>   (Proverbs 3:5–6)[8]

This passage says that you really have only two options. You can decide to trust what God has said about life and how to handle it, or you can trust yourself and come up with your own ways of handling life's challenges and finding fulfillment.

There is no third option. You are either turning to God or turning to Self in every choice in life. You think that drugs, porn, self-starvation, or alcohol will solve your problems, but they end up creating more problems for you. God says in Jeremiah 2:13 that when we turn to ourselves, we commit two evils:

> for my people have committed two evils:
> they have forsaken me,
>   the fountain of living waters,
> and [dug] cisterns for themselves,
>   broken cisterns that can hold no water.[9]

God says the first "evil" is that his people choose to turn away from him, the only source of satisfaction for thirsty souls. The second "evil" is that they choose to come up with an alternative way (which God calls a "cistern") to satisfy their "soul thirst." The problem is that these are broken cisterns that can't hold anything that is truly spiritually thirst-quenching.

God calls forsaking him "evil." Turning away from evil begins with repentance. You can't merely regret past actions; you must turn back to God and away from sin with no intention to return to your sin again. Repentance involves confessing and forsaking the sin (Proverbs 28:13). Talk to your pastor or a trusted and wise Christian friend who can show you from the Bible how to navigate all that is involved in repenting of your sin and being reconciled to God and others.

2
A Biblical Understanding of Addiction

Before a plumber can fix a pipe he has to know the composition of the pipe material—copper, PVC plastic, and so on. Each kind of pipe requires a different remedy when it leaks.

In the same way, you cannot find an adequate answer to your addiction until you know some things about your own composition and design as a human being. Your problem is more than physical, though your body is involved. Your problem isn't mental illness, though your mind is involved. Your problem goes much deeper. Your addiction has its roots in who you are.

You Are an Image-Bearing Creation of God

The Bible says,

> God created man in his own image.
>
> (Genesis 1:27)

God made you similar to himself in many ways. He made you a *rational* being like himself, so that you could think his thoughts after him and come to the same conclusions about life that he does. He also made you a *relational* being like himself, so that you could enjoy friendship with him and with human creatures like yourself. He made you a *moral* being like himself, so that you could know right from wrong and value justice. And he made you a *spiritual* being like himself, so that you could live with him forever. But something happened in the garden of Eden after Adam and Eve were created that affected every part of you.

You Are a Vandalized Creation of God

Satan wanted to rule the creation in God's place, but being a created being himself, he couldn't overpower God to get what he wanted. So, after he fell, in an attempt to get back at God he conceived a plan to vandalize the image of God in man. Satan wanted human beings to rebel against God and thus begin a journey to their own destruction—eventually death. He wanted them to imitate his own evil nature rather than God's. Jesus told us the essence of that nature in John 8:44. When addressing the evil religious leaders of his day, Jesus said,

*You are of your father the devil, and your
will is to do your father's desires. He was
a murderer from the beginning, and does
not stand in the truth, because there is no
truth in him. When he lies, he speaks out
of his own character, for he is a liar and the
father of lies.*

The more we rebel against God the more we
take on the two core characteristics of Satan
himself. We become liars or *deceivers* and are
more easily deceived ourselves because we
reject God's truth. We also become murderers or
destroyers. Our choices "murder" the prospects of
good relationships, promising opportunities, and
a fulfilling life. Satan weaves this deception and
destruction into every addiction we develop.

Satan's Pack of Lies

So how did Satan accomplish this destruction?
*Satan lied to Adam and Eve, and they believed
him!* God had told them not to eat of the fruit
of the Tree of Knowledge of Good and Evil, and
that if they did eat it, they would die. Satan told
them they would not die. He also deceived them
into believing that God was not being good to

them. He told them that God was withholding something from them because God didn't want them to become like him. Guess what! They were already like him—made in his image! Satan also told them that they really needed this fruit in order to become wise. The truth was that if they rebelled against God, they would become *unwise*!

Think carefully about what happened that day in the garden of Eden, because *every fall repeats what happened in the garden*. Here's how God described the fall in Genesis 3:1–6 when Satan, disguised as a serpent, spoke to Eve:

> Now the serpent was more crafty than any other beast of the field that the LORD God had made.
>
> He said to the woman, "Did God actually say, 'You shall not eat of any tree in the garden'?" And the woman said to the serpent, "We may eat of the fruit of the trees in the garden, but God said, 'You shall not eat of the fruit of the tree that is in the midst of the garden, neither shall you touch it, lest you die.'" But the serpent said to the woman, "You will not surely die. For God knows that when you eat of it your eyes will be opened, and you will be like God,

knowing good and evil." So when the woman
saw that the tree was good for food, and that
it was a delight to the eyes, and that the tree
was to be desired to make one wise, she took
of its fruit and ate, and she also gave some to
her husband who was with her, and he ate.

The arch liar had deceived them! Rather than being made wise they became fools. Rather than becoming like God they became more *un*like God. And because Adam fell we all fell. In Romans 5:12, the apostle Paul said,

sin came into the world through one man
[Adam], and death through sin, and so
death spread to all men because all sinned.

Our resulting sinful nature, which the Bible also calls our "flesh," mimics Satan's own nature. Our flesh wants to have its own way and push God out of our thoughts. In other words, our flesh desires independence from God and full control of our lives. The existence of our sinful nature creates an enormous conflict. Here's how Paul described it in himself in Romans 7:18–25:

For I know that nothing good dwells in me,

*that is, in my flesh. For I have the desire to
do what is right, but not the ability to carry
it out. For I do not do the good I want [to
do], but the evil I do not want [to do] is
what I keep on doing. Now if I do what I do
not want, it is no longer I [the new person
in Christ]¹⁰ who do it, but sin that dwells
within me.*

*So I find it to be a [principle] that when I
want to do right, evil lies close at hand. For I
delight in the law of God, in my inner being,
but I see in my members another law waging
war against the law of my mind and making
me captive to the [principle] of sin that
dwells in my members. Wretched man that
I am! Who will deliver me from this body
of death? Thanks be to God through Jesus
Christ our Lord! So then, I myself serve the
law of God with my mind, but with my flesh
I serve the law of sin.*

That's quite a battle! Though you are still an
image-bearer of God you have been seriously
vandalized by the fall. Now you are engaged in a
constant war between God and your own sinful
nature. Your *mind* naturally does not think as God
thinks. Your unpleasant *emotions* motivate you to

seek relief in any way you can get it, even if that way is sinful. And your *will* is instinctively committed to pleasing yourself, rather than pleasing God. So, you see, everything about your heart—your mind, emotions, and will—is corrupted.

You will never have freedom from the slavery of addiction if you do not recognize that this spiritual battle between you and God is about the control of your life. You must recognize the battle and repent every time you resist God.

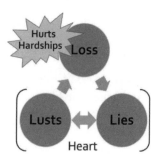

You Must Learn to Recognize Losses, Lies, and Lusts

Though Adam and Eve thought they would gain only good by eating the fruit, Satan's bait-and-switch left them with only losses. The losses at the top of the above diagram are the hurts, hardships, and uncomfortable feelings you experience on a fallen planet. The bracketed bottom portion of the diagram—lies and lusts—represents the battle that goes on inside your heart in response to your losses. Let's look at these components individually.

LOSSES

James, the half-brother of Jesus, starts chapter 1 of his book by reminding us that since we now live on a fallen planet, we will face trials of all sorts:

> *Count it all joy, my brothers, when you meet trials of various kinds, for you know that the testing of your faith produces [endurance]. And let [endurance] have its full effect, that you may be perfect and complete, lacking in nothing.*
>
> (James 1:2–4)

James rightly assumes that *everyone's life is full of trials*—setbacks, challenges, disappointments, tragedies, uncertainties, vulnerabilities, injustices, traumas, and temptations.

All of these trials produce *losses* of some sort— loss of property, loss of respect from others, loss of certainty, loss of money, loss of health, loss of valued relationships, loss of opportunities, loss of productivity, loss of our hopes and dreams, loss of joy—the list could go on and on. Whenever we experience a loss we naturally feel empty or sad.

James reminds us in these verses, however, that God can use those challenges to further restore his image in us if we will cooperate with him. That's why James says that if we work through the trial with God's wisdom we can work toward becoming "perfect [mature] and complete, lacking in nothing" (1:4).

James not only *assumes* that we will face trouble, but also *describes* the downward path of our hearts and the eventual outcome of our choices if we don't face those trials God's way:

> But each person is tempted when he is
> lured and enticed by his own desire. Then
> desire when it has conceived gives birth to
> sin, and sin when it is fully grown brings
> forth death.
>
> (1:14–15)

You must understand this passage well if you are going to beat your temptations and life-dominating sins at their core. Let's look at four lessons from these two verses.

Lesson 1: Behind Every Fall Is the Pull of Our Desires—
Sometimes Called *Lusts* in the Bible

Because losses make us feel empty or sad we immediately start looking for something to make us feel better. We don't understand how a personal relationship with Jesus could provide that joy. So we set our sights on something in this world that we think will satisfy us and make us happy.

A young man named Daniel told me that his biggest temptation was to sell cocaine, quickly assuring me that he hadn't started yet. When I asked him why he *wanted* to be a dealer he replied, "I *want* a fast car and nice clothes." "But why a fast car and nice clothes?" I asked him. After a few moments he replied, "I *want* respect."

Daniel certainly needed to reject any notion of selling cocaine and to repent of his willingness to profit from the downfall of others, but unless Daniel faced the driving lust of his heart, he would start selling cocaine or doing something else to get the money he *wanted* to gain the respect he *lusted after*.[11] A lust is often a natural human desire that has been supersized by wrong thinking or is being gratified by disobeying God.

When you do drugs, repeat the cutting, binge on food again, or sneak back into porn, you must ask yourself, "What am I *wanting* so badly that I'm willing to disobey God to get it? What am I thinking will make me happy instead of a relationship with God? How am I like Eve right now?" You may need someone to help you think through the various layers of your desires/lusts, as I had to do with Daniel, but *unless you are honest about what you really want, you can't successfully battle your sinful habits.* Sheer willpower won't cut it.

Sometimes our emotions help us figure out what we desire most. When someone or something interferes with what we want, we usually have an *emotional* reaction. To help you identify what you want most, ask yourself questions like these:

» *"Under what circumstances am I most likely to get* angry?" Phil gets angry and sometimes violent when his wife and children can't anticipate or don't do exactly what he wants. He lusts for *control* over people and over the events in his life.

» *"Under what circumstances am I most likely to become* fearful?" Sandra was sexually abused by her brother as a child and was ridiculed and finally abandoned by her husband as an adult. Sandra desperately fears rejection and longs for *safety*, *acceptance*, and *love*. She wants so badly for someone to really *love* her. She sits in loneliness at home because she fears developing friendships with people who might hurt her again.

» *"Under what circumstances am I most likely to* despair *and want to give up?"* Randy grew up with a hypercritical, perfectionistic dad. Randy felt as if he could never please his dad. He hasn't been able to keep a job as an adult because he quits work when his boss asks him to change the way he is doing the job or when he doesn't get the *approval* he craves from his employer.

In each of these cases, the person very much desires something. There is certainly nothing wrong with a desire for certainty, safety, acceptance, or approval unless it is driven by pride, inflated by discontented thinking, or pursued in a sinful way.

You will not be able to understand why you fall into temptation so easily until you begin to discover what it is that you really *want*. God says that *temptation starts with strong desires—lusts.*

Lesson 2: Behind Every Fall Is Belief in a *Lie*

Adam and Eve had a desire to be wiser, but rather than getting wisdom from God they listened to the serpent who lied to them. You must identify the desires—the *lusts*—that motivate you to do what you do, but you must also begin to identify the *lies* you are believing which keep leading you back into sinful choices.

First, you must ask yourself, *"What lies am I believing about God himself?"* Lies like these will keep you away from God, whose help you need:

- » "God can't love me after all I've done."

- » "God doesn't really love me, or he wouldn't have let my best friend die of cancer."

- » "God is the one who let my life get messed up. Why should I trust him?"

- » "I don't think God even notices me."

- » "God plays favorites, and I don't think I'll ever get on his good side."

- » "I've found out that you can't trust anyone— not even God."

Second, you must ask yourself, *"What lies am I believing about myself?"* Lies like these will keep you from admitting that you need to take responsibility and must change:

» "I know what is best for my life. I don't need other people telling me what to do."

» "I can't help it. It's not my fault that I don't handle alcohol as well as my friends."

» "It's my body. I can do with it what I please, so get off my case!"

» "One more time won't hurt. I'll quit after this time."

» "I can handle this. I've got everything under control."

» "All of this is too hard. I may as well give up!"

» "God made me this way. It's genetic."

» "You can't expect me to endure this emotional pain. I have a right to do whatever I need to do to feel better."

» "I don't need other people. I do better on my own."

Third, you must ask yourself, *"What lies am I believing about the way God's world works?"* God's world is a moral universe, and he has told us what is right and wrong in his Word, the Bible. Thoughts like these allow you to justify your disobedience to God:

- » "Everybody else is doing it, so what does it matter?"

- » "You haven't been through the same thing I have, so you can't understand me or tell me what to do."

- » "As long as I have confidence in myself and feel good about myself, I'm OK."

- » "What's wrong with a little pleasure? God wants me to have a good time, doesn't he?"

- » "I don't have to apologize to other people for my wrong behavior if they don't deserve the apology."

A lie is essentially a "contradiction of reality." Satan uses the lies you hear from the world around you and the lies that your own sinful heart generates to keep you in slavery. Jesus said in John 8:32 that the only way out of sin's slavery is to know truth:

> you will know the truth, and the truth will set you free.

The only source of absolute truth is the Bible— God's Word. *You cannot be free from life-dominating sins if you are not continually learning, believing, and obeying truth from the Bible.* Therefore, you need a spiritually minded mentor, a Bible-preaching pastor, or friends who know the Bible to help you sort out the lies that have kept you enslaved.

Lesson 3: Behind Every Fall Is a *Choice* to Believe Lies and Satisfy Your Lust for Relief or Joy/Pleasure in Your Own Way

Remember how the temptation in the garden of Eden unfolded in Genesis 3:6?

> So when the woman saw that the tree was good for food [*she desired its benefit of flavor and nourishment*], and that it was a delight to the eyes [*she was attracted to its beauty*], and that the tree was to be desired to make one wise [*she desired its benefit of increased wisdom*], she took of its fruit and ate, and she also gave some to her husband who was with her, and he ate.

She fell because she thought the fruit would give her something she *desired*. She *believed the lies* of Satan that she would only profit from the experience and that there would be no downside. Once she believed the lies, the next step was to *disobey* God and take the fruit. She did not consult God, but "followed her heart," and fell into sin. It might seem to us that her eating the fruit was a very small thing, but the effects for her, Adam, and all of us were catastrophic. Satan had trapped her.

Lesson 4: Repeated Sin Leads to the *Death* of Something
James 1:15 says that

> sin when it is fully grown brings forth death.

Every time we sin, something begins to die. Look at Figure 1 again and notice that once you make decisions based upon *lies* and sinful *lusts*, you generate more *losses* for yourself, and the cycle starts all over again. Think about these realities:

» Eventually, you seem to lose your *ability to choose*; choice seems to die, and an addiction is born. Life seems to be driven by triggers and cravings. Although you are never without the ability to choose, it certainly feels as if you don't have a choice. You are losing your freedom.

» Certainly, you lose your ability to choose the *consequences* of your actions. Someone has said that you are free to choose your sin, but you are not free to choose the consequences of your sin. Life-dominating sins have many deadly consequences—death of your health, death of your employment, death of your financial situation, death of relationships, death of your emotional well-being, and death of hope. Eve thought she would really "live" when she chose to eat the fruit, but she was sorely disappointed.

All of these "deaths" unfold because God promised that they would. He said that "sin when it is fully grown brings forth death." You can already see that to get out of the slavery, you must start thinking differently. You must identify the *losses* that are painful to think about and learn how God wants you to handle them. You must identify the *lusts* or desires you pursue in order to relieve your pain. You must reject the *lies* that keep you enslaved, and you must learn to walk in *repentance* and *dependence* upon God. Let's look at the kind of person God will help you become so that you can have lasting freedom, satisfaction, and fulfillment.

3

God's Roadmap to Freedom

Imagine what your life would be like:

» If you had joy so that you weren't always looking for some other way to feel better;

» If you knew what God would want you to do because you were well acquainted with the example of Jesus;

» If you had the power through God to have self-control; or

» If you could stand under pressure with God's help.

Would that change the way you handle the trials of life? Would that make a difference in how you handle losses, counter lies, and resist your lusts? Of course it would!

Breaking the hold that sin has on your life and handling losses wisely come through maturing in your Christian walk. Mature Christians are tempted to sin, and mature Christians do sin. But mature Christians are not dominated by sin, because they are learning to respond to hurts and hardships God's way. We could say that *God's recovery program is sanctification*—Christian growth. This is the emphasis in Freedom That Lasts.

Freedom That Lasts

Freedom That Lasts (FTL) is a Christ-centered, discipleship-based, local-church ministry to those enslaved to life-dominating sins or overcome by hurtful events of life. My wife and I started this ministry at our church in 2010 when God began bringing more and more addicted men and women across our paths. The local chapter at our church ministers to 75–100 men and women every Friday night, as I write this mini-book at the start of 2020.

Each week, when I speak to a small group of those who are attending FTL for the first time, I tell them that they will seldom hear me speak of *sobriety*, though we are thankful for anyone who achieves it. I tell them that

> *our goal goes far beyond sobriety, because*
> *you can be clean and sober and still be*
> *miserable; you can be clean and sober and*
> *still be a thief; you can be clean and sober*

*and still be an adulterer. You can't be like
Jesus, however, and be any of those things.
So, we are going to focus on these Friday
night classes and in the curriculum on how
we can know and become more like Jesus.*

Our program focuses on evangelism and on
the Bible's teaching about "progressive sanctification"—a biblical term for changing and
growing to be like Jesus Christ. Each Friday night
we recite aloud together our "change principle,"
which emphasizes change from the inside out:

*You do what you do because you are what
you are. To change what you do, you must
cooperate with God to change what you are.*

We also recite together our motto:

*Jesus Christ is the only source of freedom
that lasts.*

I remind them that

*freedom isn't found in a program—
not even Freedom That Lasts—or in a
resident facility or in a relationship* unless

*that program, facility, or relationship
intentionally points you to Jesus Christ.*

Freedom from life-dominating sins and stubborn habits begins with a personal, growing relationship with the person of Jesus Christ and with a commitment to develop his character as an image-bearer.

If as you read this mini-book you are not sure that you personally know Jesus Christ, please talk to the person who gave you this book or seek out someone who can show you from the Bible how you can know Jesus Christ personally as your own Lord and Savior from sin.[12] Freedom from any life-dominating sin always starts with a saving relationship with Jesus Christ.

A Relationship with Jesus Christ Is the Only Source of Lasting Joy and Peace

If you have ever seriously dated or been engaged, you may remember thinking, "I know we don't have a lot of money, a fancy apartment, or nice furniture, but we don't need anything else as long as we have each other!" What God allowed you to experience then, if only in a small way, is the fact that you were made to find joy and satisfaction in relationship—most importantly, in relationship with Jesus Christ. He said in John 15:11,

> These things I have spoken to you, that my joy may be in you, and that your joy may be full.

The apostle Paul said that God would produce the fruit of *joy* and *peace* in us as we live in fellowship with God (Galatians 5:22). You have been trying to find elevated emotions, relief, and peace from your inner turmoil through substances or behaviors. Those are temporary, counterfeit joys and peace. They bring death instead of life. Jesus has so much more for you, but you must learn to develop a personal, growing relationship with him.

If you employ a personal trainer in a gym you soon learn much about your coach as you listen to the coach talk about his or her life and as you talk to the coach about your life. Peter says that if you will spend time with God to develop your spiritual character you will develop an intimate relationship with Jesus (2 Peter 1:8) because you will listen to him in his Word and talk to him in prayer. If you lack joy and peace you must get back into fellowship with Jesus and cooperate with him as he develops his character in you.

Developing the Character of Jesus Christ Is the Only Source of True Freedom

The apostle Peter doesn't leave us to wonder what the character of Jesus looks like. In fact, Peter's list of virtues in 2 Peter 1:5–10 is probably the most complete portrait of Christlikeness anywhere in the Bible.[13] Here is Peter's list and a promise from God when we work to develop them:

> make every effort *to supplement your* [saving] *faith* with *virtue*, and virtue with *knowledge*, and knowledge with *self-control*, and self- control with [*endurance*], and [*endurance*] with *godliness*, and godliness with *brotherly affection*, and brotherly affection with *love* . . . for if you practice these qualities you will never fall.

Peter is not saying in verse 10 that we will never sin, but that we won't become stuck in the quicksand of our sin as we have been before.

I want to explain to you the virtues in this Bible passage and show you how growth toward Christian maturity is the path to freedom from your life-dominating sins and stubborn habits.

Saving faith is "believing that Jesus Christ is

my only Savior."[14] You cannot have a stable and spiritually satisfying life without the foundation of saving faith. You must know for sure that you are God's child, that your sins are forgiven, and that you are spiritually alive, so that you can begin to grow to be more like Christ. But salvation is just the start. There is so much more! Peter lists seven virtues that we are to cultivate in our character once we know Jesus Christ through saving faith. They are necessary for victory over the hurts and addictions of life on a broken planet.

1. *Cultivating virtue* means "being committed to developing and displaying the character of Jesus Christ." Peter refers to a certain kind of virtue—the excellent character of Jesus.

   Change starts with commitment to developing that excellence. If you wanted to lose some pounds or develop your heart and lungs you would need to commit yourself to changing your eating or to beginning an exercise program. So many Christian recovery programs and efforts fail at this point. They try to add self-control to people who haven't decided they want to be like Jesus in the first place. Maturing as a Christian starts with an ongoing commitment to become more like Jesus Christ with the Spirit's help.

2. *Cultivating knowledge* means "knowing the person, words, and ways of Jesus Christ." Knowing Jesus Christ includes both knowing him in a personal relationship and knowing things about him. The apostle Paul said in Romans 15:13 that knowing and believing God's Word is also the road to *joy* and *peace*—and these together make up the essence of contentment:

May the God of hope fill you with all joy and peace in believing, so that by the power of the Holy Spirit you may abound in hope.

Earlier you learned that Satan's primary weapon against you is his lies about God, about yourself, and about the way God's world works.

Often addicted believers get "clean and sober" at a resident facility or with the help of loved ones, but then relapse—fall again—when they face trouble weeks or months later. They are especially vulnerable if they haven't *learned to go to God in prayer* when they need help, haven't *replaced the lies they believe with God's truth*, and haven't *replaced their selfish desires with godly desires*. They haven't been cultivating "knowledge" about God and his ways.

We need truth to counter lies, but we also need truth to teach us how we ought to live life. Addicts are warned about triggers— stress, former places where they hung out, and people with whom they did drugs or had sex. The book of Proverbs provides teaching for many of these matters. The Bible calls this kind of truth "wisdom." You must begin a diligent pursuit of God's wisdom in his Word, the Bible. Maturing Christians read, study, meditate upon, and memorize verses in their Bibles.

3. *Cultivating self-control* means "instantly obeying God's Word in the power of God's Spirit." From the standpoint of the Bible, self-control is Spirit-control. Notice, in the verses below, the contrast between obeying your fleshly desires and obeying the Spirit of God:

But I say, walk by the Spirit, and you will not gratify the desires of the flesh.

(Galatians 5:16)

And do not get drunk with wine, for that is debauchery, but be filled with the Spirit.

(Ephesians 5:18)

If you have been dominated by sin in your life, you have been living by your feelings and impulses, not by the principles and commands of God from his Word.

4. *Cultivating endurance* means "continuing to obey God's Word in the power of God's Spirit no matter what." Self-control means battling the *internal* battles of our flesh. Endurance often involves staying faithful to God and his ways in the face of extended *external* pressures. Those pressures might be peer pressure, work pressure, financial pressure, relational pressure, or health pressure.

Just as physical muscles cannot be developed without exercising them against some form of resistance, you won't develop spiritual endurance without facing some sort of trial and pressure. Pressures mature us when we respond to them with wisdom from God and with a heart committed to obeying God no matter what (James 1:4–8; Hebrews 12:1–3).

Imagine what your life would be like if you faithfully said "no" to the appeals of ungodly people and the world around you, or if you consistently made financial or relational decisions based upon scriptural principles even when pressured to cave in.

5. *Cultivating godliness* means "loving Jesus Christ with my whole heart and promoting and defending what is important to him." If you are committed to becoming like Jesus, to growing in your knowledge of Jesus and his ways, to battling your flesh with Spirit-control, and to enduring even under pressure from others, some of your friends and family may think you are too "religious." They might even make fun of you (2 Timothy 3:12), but godliness strengthens us to be loyal to Jesus no matter what.

Can you see why you would need endurance in order to handle the pressure of others' scorn when you follow Jesus wholeheartedly? Self-control, endurance, and godliness are the backbone or strength of your Christian character.

6-7. *Cultivating brotherly affection* means "showing special concern for my brothers and sisters in Christ," and *cultivating love* means "sacrificing to meet the spiritual needs of others." When we develop these virtues, we start caring for others, and we start forgetting about ourselves. We find fulfillment in helping others and stop focusing so much on our own problems.

We All Need Transformation, Not Mere Recovery

Do you remember the change principle we looked at earlier?

> *You do what you do because you are what you are. To change what you do, you must cooperate with God to change what you are.*

That change principle reminds us that God offers us far more than recovery or sobriety can offer. He offers us transformation of our character as we seek to know, love, and obey God (Romans 12:1–2; Ephesians 4:22–24).[15]

4
Freedom Applications

As we saw in the first chapter, you are an embodied soul, created in the image of God. Both your body and your soul—your heart—were seriously damaged in the fall. But your choices have contributed further damage to both. I want to illustrate the journey back to physical health and spiritual change and growth with a baseball metaphor.

Humility Is First Base

Jesus is God in human, bodily form. If you were to see a human being who is totally like God in every way, as Jesus is, one of the most dominant characteristics of that person would be humility. In our Friday night Freedom That Lasts class, I often remind us all that "humility is first base" in the Christian life. Humility is the frame of mind you have when you take your rightful place in submission to God. Humility has several manifestations that you must cultivate to be free from the slavery of sin.

First, humility manifests itself in *repentance*. Humble people no longer hide their sin, blame others for their sin, or rationalize their sin. Humble people turn their backs on their sin and turn their face to God in submission and obedience. They stop lying and start living in reality. They know that they sinned and that they need forgiveness from God and from others. Listen to God's appeal to the children of Israel who were headed to slavery under foreign nations if they did not return to God:

> Seek the LORD while he may be found;
>   call upon him while he is near;
> let the wicked forsake his way,
>   and the unrighteous man his thoughts;
> let him return to the LORD, that he may have
>   compassion on him,
>   and to our God, for he will abundantly pardon.
>   (Isaiah 55:6–7)

God is saying, "You must see that you have forsaken me in your quest for something to satisfy your thirst. You must return to me in repentance for going your own way and for thinking your own thoughts. You can be sure that I will abundantly pardon your waywardness. I am a God who delights in mercy!"

Is this a step you need to take? If so, what must you "confess and forsake" (Proverbs 28:13)? If you are not sure how to get started, are you willing to *humble* yourself and talk to your pastor or to a mature Christian counselor or friend who will compassionately but firmly tell you what you need to hear and direct you to God's Word for answers?

Second, humility is manifested in *dependence*. As we saw earlier, God made us to be dependent creatures. We were made to need God and his words. We were made to need other Christians. Sin separates us from God and from others.

Your need for help as you break free of your sinful habits may be so great that you have to get help in a biblically based resident addiction-recovery facility.[16] This may seem like an impossibility for you because it will take you out of your job, and maybe your family, for six months to a year. But if you are honest with yourself, you will admit that you are going to need at least that much time to unpack all the lies and lusts you have been harboring and to be "transformed by the renewal of your mind" (Romans 12:2).

Beyond the humility to enter a resident facility you will need humility to become a member of a

Bible-preaching local church where you will be fed from God's Word, will find the encouragement you need in your struggles, and will find the accountability you need for your life through godly mentors and a godly pastoral staff.

You were made to be part of a local flock of God's sheep overseen by one or more of God's shepherds who take their responsibility seriously. Lone sheep are easy prey to wolves. You must stay connected as a member of a Gospel-centered, Bible-preaching local church. Don't just drift from one church to another. *You need to belong somewhere*. I have found that in our Freedom That Lasts chapter, the participants who join a church, submit to wise counsel and accountability, and worship weekly with the church body become stable and fruitful. The lone sheep who wants to develop his or her "own recovery plan" doesn't make it. God made us to be *dependent*. Be humble enough to admit it and live like it.

Hearing Is Second Base

All the students working the Freedom That Lasts curriculum memorize Matthew 7:24–27 where Jesus ended his first sermon, the one we call the "Sermon on the Mount," with these words about hearing:

*Everyone then who hears these words of
mine and does them will be like a wise man
who built his house on the rock. And the
rain fell, and the floods came, and the winds
blew and beat on that house, but it did not
fall, because it had been founded on the
rock. And everyone who hears these words
of mine and does not do them will be like
a foolish man who built his house on the
sand. And the rain fell, and the floods came,
and the winds blew and beat against that
house, and it fell, and great was the fall of it.*

One manifestation of first base humility and its
quality of *dependence* is that the follower of Jesus
is willing to *hear* the words of God.

Hearing God's Word means reading your Bible,
memorizing key Bible verses, listening to Bible-
centered preaching at your local church, reading
books to help you grow as a Christian, and perhaps
becoming a part of a small group Bible study.

You must see that your freedom from sin and
your stability in life are found in a relationship
with Jesus Christ. Jesus said, "Everyone . . .
who hears these words of *mine*." Your first
job is to develop your relationship with Jesus
Christ by listening to *him*, talking to *him*, and

committing yourself to obedience to *him*.

Doing Is Third Base

In the verses we just looked at in Matthew 7, Jesus says that there are some people who regularly "hear" God's Word but won't "do" it. Jesus says that when the storms of life return, these people fall. The following will help you "do" the right thing when you are triggered or tempted.

When you are tempted, you cannot ignore the Holy Spirit's conviction and pretend that God doesn't exist or doesn't care about what you are about to do. Sometimes a child will stick his fingers in his ears, shake his head, and say, "la-la-la-la . . ." in order to drown out the words of someone he doesn't want to listen to. You cannot be like that child and turn away from God. You must turn *to* God at the first thought of temptation. If you entertain the idea of your old habit for any amount of time, you will likely give in to it!

1. Immediately stop and pray something like this: "Jesus, I'm facing trouble right now, and I don't want to hurt my relationship with you. You want me to turn away from this temptation, and I want to listen to you."

2. Tell God you are believing his promises. For example, "You have told me that 'I can do all things through him who strengthens me' (Philippians 4:13). I believe your Word and am asking you for that strength to obey you right now."

3. Move away from the temptation in some way: "Jesus, I think the wisest thing for me right now is to [leave the room/call my mentor/shut down my computer or phone, etc.], so that's what I'm doing right now. Thank you for helping me obey you!"

Wisdom and Freedom Are Home Plate

Did you notice in Jesus' words (Matthew 7:24–27) that the one who hears his words and does them will be a stable, wise person? Wisdom is skill at living; wisdom is seeing all of life from God's perspective and submitting yourself to his ways. Living wisely is the key to pursuing and experiencing freedom and fulfillment.

Conclusion

If you picked up this mini-book because you are enslaved to a life-dominating sin or stubborn habit, or you have experienced serious losses and hurts, I hope you have a clearer picture of the spiritual battle going on behind the scenes within your heart. The sinful *lusts* of your heart, coupled with the *lies* you have believed, have led you into a trap that is destroying you.

I hope that you also have a better picture of what it means to give serious consideration to your spiritual life, even though your addiction may feel as if it is something entirely physical. Let me assure you, it is not. You certainly may need detox and medical attention for the effects of your addiction. If that is the case, admit your problem and seek out that help.

But your deliverance is going to come from a Person—Jesus Christ! He appeals to you in Matthew 11:28–29:

> *Come to me, all who labor and are heavy laden, and I will give you rest. Take my yoke [of discipleship] upon you, and learn from me . . . and you will find rest for your souls.*

This is a wonderful invitation! Jesus wants you to come to him in humility. He wants you to learn from him so that you can become like him.

Why would Jesus make that promise to you? It is because he is thinking of you. He died and rose again to free you from sin and he loves you. Humble yourself and get into his yoke of discipleship. You'll never regret it.

Personal Application Projects

We talked much about losses, lies, and lusts in chapter 2. Read that chapter again and answer these questions.

1. What are the losses in your life that you have a hard time handling—loss of property, respect from others, certainty, money, health, valued relationships, opportunities, productivity, hopes and dreams, a clear conscience because of guilt . . . ? Write them down. Ask a mature Christian to help you find biblical principles and promises from God that will help you to handle those losses in a biblical way.

2. Losses always make us feel bad, so we start desiring things that we think will make us feel better and give us relief. Go back and answer the questions in chapter 2, Lesson 1. Read through the examples and write out your own answers to these questions to help you identify your ruling lusts:

- » Under what circumstances am I most likely to get *angry*?

- » Under what circumstances am I most likely to become *fearful*?

- » Under what circumstances am I most likely to *despair* and want to give up?

What are your ruling desires—the lusts—that keep pulling you back into sinful ways? Again, ask a mature Christian to help you find Bible principles for saying "no" to these desires and for developing desires that honor God.

3. In chapter 2, Lesson 2, we learned that "behind every fall is belief in a lie." Again, read through the examples in that section and answer these questions:

- » What lies am I believing about *God himself*?

- » What lies am I believing about *myself*?

- » What lies am I believing about *the way God's world works*?

4. In chapter 2, Lesson 3, we learned that "behind every fall is a *choice* to believe lies and satisfy your lust . . . in your own way." Since these choices defy God, you must repent of them. Make a list of the choices you have made in disobedience to God. Ask God to forgive you for each one and seek the help of a mature Christian to make restitution and reconciliation with those you have hurt or taken advantage of along the way.

5. Lastly, you must become serious about loving and developing the character of Christ. Those who learn to think like Jesus are on the pathway to developing joy and peace (Galatians 5:22). Review chapters 3 and 4 to see what Jesus' character looks like and begin studying some of the materials in the "Where Can I Get More Help?" section that follows.

Where Can I Get More Help?

BOOKS ON ADDICTION

Dunham, David R., *Addictive Habits: Changing for Good* (Phillipsburg, NJ: P&R, 2018).

Shaw, Mark, *Divine Intervention: Hope and Help for Families of Addicts* (Bemidji, MN: Focus, 2011).

———, *The Heart of Addiction: A Biblical Perspective* (Bemidji, MN: Focus, 2008).

Welch, Edward T., *Addictions: A Banquet in the Grave* (Phillipsburg, NJ: P&R, 2001).

BOOKS BY THE AUTHOR ON CHRISTIAN GROWTH

Berg, Jim, *Changed into His Image: God's Plan for Transforming Your Life*, 2nd ed. (Greenville, SC: JourneyForth, 2018).

———, *Essential Virtues: Marks of the Christ-Centered Life* (Greenville, SC: JourneyForth, 2008).

WEBSITES THAT OFFER BIBLICAL HELP FOR ADDICTION

Freedom That Lasts: www.freedomthatlasts.com

The author's website: www.jimberg.com

The Addiction Connection: www.theaddictionconnection.org

Counseling resources on addiction from IBCD: www.ibcd.org/topics/addictions/

The author's training seminar for FTL volunteers: www.udemy.com/course/helping-others-overcome-addictions/

Endnotes

1 Names and details in this book have been changed to protect the identities of those concerned.

2 www.freedomthatlasts.com.

3 American Society of Addiction Medicine (ASAM), "Definition of Addiction," www.asam.org/resources/definition-of-addiction.

4 Marc Lewis, PhD, *The Biology of Desire: Why Addiction Is Not a Disease* (New York: PublicAffairs, 2015), xi.

5 Ibid., x.

6 Edward T. Welch, *Addictions: A Banquet in the Grave* (Phillipsburg, NJ: P&R, 2001), 46.

7 I use the word "disorder" not as a psychiatric label but only to draw attention to the fact that your life is "out of order."

8 All Scripture quotations are from the English Standard Version (ESV). Any bracketed words either substitute another word or explain a word for clarity.

9 A cistern in Bible times was an underground plastered pit dug to catch and hold rainwater; they often leaked.

10 2 Corinthians 5:17 says, "Therefore, if anyone is in Christ, he is a new creation. The old has passed away; behold, the new has come."

11 Desiring respect—honor—is not necessarily sinful, but Daniel was willing to get it in his own way in violation of God's laws. God tells us that the way to gain honor is to earn it (John 12:24–26).

12 You can watch a twenty-minute video telling you how to have this kind of relationship with God at https://vimeo.com/232509956.

13 For an extended study of these virtues, see my *Essential Virtues: Marks of the Christ-Centered Life* (Greenville, SC: JourneyForth, 2008). This book forms the basis for the first curriculum level of Freedom That Lasts and for this chapter.

14 Definitions for "saving faith" and for each of the virtues are from Jim Berg, *Freedom That Lasts, Level 1: Finding Freedom God's Way* (Taylors, SC: Freedom That Lasts, 2019; www.freedomthatlasts.com).

15 For help on transformation, see the "Books by the Author on Christian Growth" in the "Where Can I Get More Help?" section at the end of this mini-book.

16 Not every facility or "Christian" addiction counseling clinic uses the Bible to help you become more like Christ and learn to do spiritual battle against your flesh. Many use the Bible only for offering hope and comfort and for offering the gospel. Check out the residential programs listed at The Addiction Connection, https://www.theaddictionconnection.org/residential-programs/. The Addiction Connection is a network of individuals, resident programs, and non-resident programs that approach addiction from a biblical counseling standpoint.

www.freedomthatlasts.com

MISSION STATEMENT

Freedom That Lasts® is a Christ-centered, Bible-based, local-church-focused discipleship ministry to those enslaved in life-dominating sins or overcome by hurtful events of life.

We believe God's mission on the earth is to redeem and restore fallen people to the likeness of His Son to the praise of His glory.

In order to advance God's mission, Freedom That Lasts® is, first, an evangelistic ministry, since long-term bondage to sin often indicates a lost condition. No lasting progress can be made in overcoming life-dominating sins without saving faith in Jesus Christ.

Secondly, Freedom That Lasts® is a ministry of sanctification whereby the program staff joins God's mission to restore redeemed people to the likeness of Jesus Christ.

Never in modern history has this type of ministry been needed more. Almost every family in our communities is touched by addiction. Alcohol and drug abuse play a key role in many divorces, job losses, teen suicides, and family dysfunction. By offering an addiction ministry, a local church extends a helping hand and a gospel witness to its neighbors.

CONTACT FREEDOM THAT LASTS®

Website: www.freedomthatlasts.com

Call: 864.322.0700, ext, 1108

Email: info@freedomthatlasts.com

Books in the Help! series include...

More titles in preparation

For current listing go to: www.shepherdpress.com/lifeline

About Shepherd Press Publications

- » They are gospel driven.
- » They are heart focused.
- » They are life changing.

Our Invitation to You

We passionately believe that what we are publishing can be of benefit to you, your family, your friends, and your work colleagues. So we are inviting you to join our online mailing list so that we may reach out to you with news about our latest and forthcoming publications, and with special offers.

Visit:

www.shepherdpress.com/newsletter
and provide your name and email address.